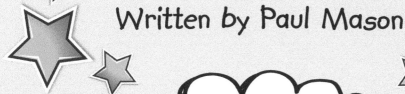

MY SKATEBOARDING SCRAPBOOK

Written by Paul Mason

Contents

MY NEW DECK

Monday 3rd September

Look at my new skateboard!

It took a long time to save up the money. I'm really pleased with it.

Board parts

deck

kicktail

nose

trucks

wheels

ZINC

REGULAR OR GOOFY?

If you ride with your left foot at the front of the skateboard, you are a regular. If you ride with your right foot in front, then you are a goofy.

Am I a regular or a goofy rider?

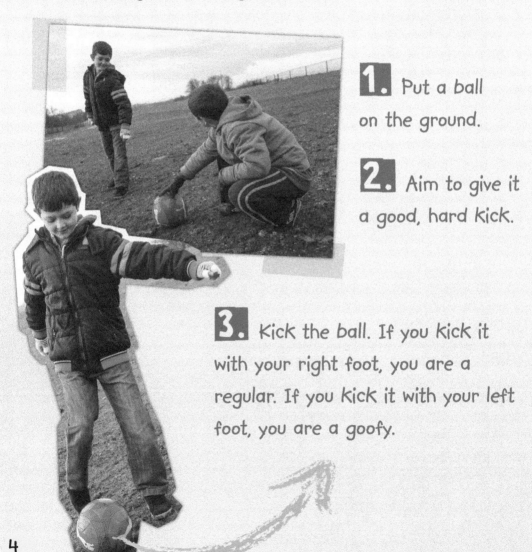

1. Put a ball on the ground.

2. Aim to give it a good, hard kick.

3. Kick the ball. If you kick it with your right foot, you are a regular. If you kick it with your left foot, you are a goofy.

Pulling yourself along a fence helps you keep your balance when you start out.

GOING DOWN A HILL

Wednesday 12th September

Today I went out skateboarding with my friend Ted. We took turns to go down a little hill.

Wicked!

1. Move any big stones out of the way.

2. Bend your knees.

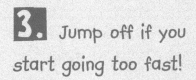

3. Jump off if you start going too fast!

One day, I might go down a slope like this!

PUSHING OFF

Wednesday 26th September

I had to work out how to move the board by pushing off with my foot. Pushing off with my back foot worked best.

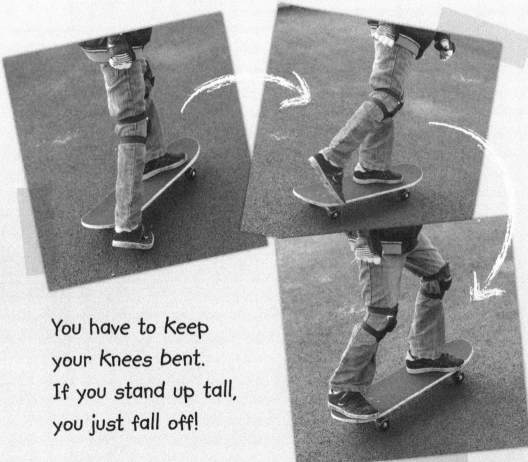

You have to keep your knees bent. If you stand up tall, you just fall off!

One day, I'll be this fast!

PUSHING-OFF GAME

Tuesday 9th October

Ted and I made up a game to get better at pushing off.

1. Draw a start line on the ground with chalk.

2. Put one foot on the deck, ready to push off.

3. Take one big push.

4. See who can make the longest push.
This time it was Ted.

When you've done it with one push,
you can try it with two, three, four
pushes or even more.

MY FIRST CRASH

Tuesday 16th October

I had my first crash today. My wheel hit a stone. The board stopped and I went flying!

My pads and helmet kept me from getting badly hurt.

helmet

elbow
pads

wrist
guards

knee
pads

TURNS

Thursday 25th October

Ted's brother showed us how to turn a skateboard.

It took a few tries to get it right!

You do it like this:

1. Bend your knees.

2. Press down on the deck so that it tips the way you want to turn.

It might be a while before I can turn this well – or go this fast!

MORE TURNS

Saturday 3rd November

Ted and I set up a little slalom course so we could do some more work on our turns.

plastic bottles filled with water

We went in and out between the bottles. We did our best skating yet!

Slalom contests

Two skaters start together side by side. The first one to finish wins the contest.

EXPERTS ONLY!

Anyone who pushes over a cone is out. Most people like to finish the course anyway.

NEW TRICKS

Saturday 17th November

Today we tried to learn some skateboard tricks. First we did kick turns.

1. Stand with your back foot on the kicktail.

2. Press down with your back foot. This lifts the front wheels off the ground.

3. Turn your shoulders to make the board spin round.

Then we tried a trick
called 'walking the dog'.

1. Put your front foot in
the middle of the deck.

2. Move your back foot
to the nose of the deck.

3. Press down on
the nose and do a
little wheelie.

4. Swing the board
round so that the nose
is at the back.

5. Start again.

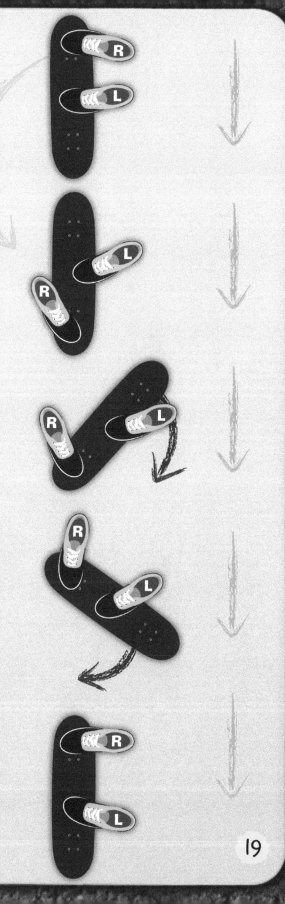

THE SKATE PARK

Wednesday 28th November

At last! Ted's dad says he's going to take us to the skate park on Saturday.

stair jump

fun box

rail

Rules of the park

1. Wear a helmet.

2. Do not go on ramps that are too difficult for you.

3. Wait your turn.

spine ramp

21

THE MINI RAMP

Sunday 2nd December

We really loved it at the skate park!
We found a mini ramp that no one
was using. We went up one side and
back down again.

Landing on your pads doesn't hurt!

In the end, we both had three goes
in a row. We were pretty good!

EXPERTS ONLY!

If I practise really hard,
maybe one day I'll do this!

Glossary

fun box	skate park kit for doing tricks
goofy	someone who skateboards with their right foot at the front of the deck
kick turn	turn done by lifting the front wheels of a skateboard off the ground and swinging them round
mini ramp	small, two-sided ramp with a flat bit between the sides
regular	someone who skateboards with their left foot at the front of the deck
slalom	race or track with lots of turns
wheelie	when the front or back wheels are lifted off the ground